362.7   Weintraub, Aileen,
WEI   1973-

in

4941

362.7
WEI

Weintraub, Aileen, 1973-
    Choosing a career in chil
Weintraub. -- 1st ed. -- New
2000.
    64 p. : ill. (some col.) ; 24 c
work)

    34880030034941 $25.25
    Includes bibliographical refer
index.
    ISBN 0-8239-3241-9 (lib. bdg.)
    1. Child care--Vocational guid
Vocational guidance. I. Title.
(New York, N.Y.)

HQ778.63.W44 2000

Enhanced MARC
008464   9703968   B SL

362.

The World of Work

Choosing a Career in Child Care

If you care deeply about the happiness and well-being of children, you
may want to explore a career in child care.

The World of Work

Choosing a Career in Child Care

Aileen Weintraub

The Rosen Publishing Group, Inc.
New York

To Grandma Mollie, for being an incredible role model.

Published in 2000 by The Rosen Publishing Group, Inc.
29 East 21st Street, New York, NY 10010

Library of Congress Cataloging-in-Publication Data

Weintraub, Aileen, 1973–
    Careers in child care / by Aileen Weintraub.
       p. cm.—(The world of work)
    Includes bibliographical references and index.
    Summary: Examines various careers for teenagers interested in working with children, as well as how to prepare for them.
    ISBN 0-8239-3241-9 (Lib. Bdg.)
    1. Child care—Vocational guidance—United States—Juvenile literature. 2. Child welfare—Vocational guidance—United States—Juvenile literature. [1. Child care—Vocational guidance. 2. Vocational guidance.] I. Title. II. World of work (New York, N.Y.).

HQ778.63.W44 2000
362.7'023—dc21

                                        99-086527

Manufactured in the United States of America

Contents

Introduction

As you grow older, you begin to figure out what types of things you are interested in doing. You start to realize what you're good at and what activities make you happy. There are many careers to choose from, and finding the right one can take time and effort. The more information and knowledge you have, the better prepared you will be to choose a fulfilling career.

There are many things to consider when choosing a career. The right job for you depends on how many hours you are willing to work, what kind of salary you are looking for, and what type of training you are willing to get.

If you like spending time with children, there are many opportunities to explore. Once you decide that working with children is right for you, you then have to decide in what way you would like to work with them. The term "child care" has a broad definition that includes many different jobs. For example, if you decide that you like working with very young children, you can explore jobs that involve working in a day care center or you can consider becoming a nanny. You may decide that you like to read to children or want to be involved in their education. In this case you can consider becoming a teacher. There are also many other jobs in child care that might not be so obvious. You may be good at relating to children and talking about things that bother them. Child psychologists and social workers are trained to do this type of work. If you like science and are interested in medicine, you can think about becoming a nurse or even a pediatrician.

Gaining experience is the best way to decide what you like and do not like. There are many ways to do this, and it is easy to begin working with children in volunteer programs, or by becoming a baby-sitter or even a tutor. Sometimes getting started can be the hardest part, but with a little research and exploration, you can find yourself on a solid path to an exciting career in the field of child care.

When you are faced with a serious career choice, it often helps to make lists of your strengths and weaknesses, likes and dislikes.

Finding the Right Job 1

"What do you want to be when you grow up?" That's a question everybody has heard at least once as a child. Some people have always known what they want to do with the rest of their lives, but most people change their minds quite a few times before settling into a career.

Graduation day was quickly approaching for Rena, and she still had no idea what type of job she wanted. She went to the school library to do some research, hoping to get a few ideas. The librarian directed her to the career section. She found a few books and started flipping through the pages. Rena began to feel overwhelmed. There were so many things to consider. Many of her friends knew exactly what they wanted to do after graduation, but she wasn't quite so sure. She did know that she wanted a job that would make her happy. One of the books suggested that she make a list of all the things she liked to do and what she expected to get out of a career.

Rena knew she was a bright girl who did well in school. She wasn't sure she wanted to go to college, but she was willing to go for training once she picked a specific career path. After making her list, she realized that she wanted to work close to home so she wouldn't have to relocate or spend too much time traveling. She also realized that she liked working with people and didn't mind long hours as long as she got enough vacation time. She also decided that a high salary wasn't that important to begin with, but she did want a job that would give her enough experience to be able to make more money down the road.

Rena still didn't know exactly what she wanted to do, but she felt more confident that with a little research she would be able to find a job that suited her well. Figuring out her basic skills and knowing what she wanted in a career helped Rena get a solid start on the road to success.

Choosing the right career can prove to be a challenge. It is hard to know what you want to do with the rest of your life. There are many things to consider before deciding on a career. A career should be meaningful, so that you get personal satisfaction out of what you are doing. It's important to enjoy what you do because a job takes up a good portion of your life. A career should also bring you financial security so that you are able to support yourself. The career you choose should be rewarding in many ways.

Finding the right job takes a lot of research and planning. This is important so you don't waste time accepting jobs you have no interest in. This is an opportunity to explore your individuality, decide what your interests and talents are, and figure out what skills you have.

Working with Children

There are a few very basic things to consider when looking for a career in child care that will help you narrow down your search. Working with kids can be challenging. Children have special needs and require a lot of patience and understanding. Kids can't always express themselves as well as adults. Before choosing a career in child care, you need to ask yourself a few questions. Children are still learning and growing and may not understand concepts that an adult might take for granted, like sharing, listening, and respecting others. Some people may find this frustrating.

Do you have the right attitude to work with kids? Are you generally a happy, creative, patient person? Do you like being around children even when they are noisy or angry? Are you kind and understanding? Are you responsible enough to care for a child? Do you enjoy working with large groups of children, or do you prefer working with just a few at a time?

A good way to find out if you are right for a career in child care is to make two columns on a piece of paper. One column should list your positive personality traits, like being cheerful or funny. The other column should list reasons why you want to work with kids. This will help you determine if you have the right personality to deal with children and if you have valid reasons for wanting to work with them. For example, do you want to work with kids just because you think it would be fun, or because you can contribute something meaningful to a child's life?

Education and Training

Having a high school diploma is important when applying for jobs. The first thing you need to decide is how much schooling you plan to have. Are you willing to take special classes in your field of interest? Sometimes jobs have training programs to help you learn the skills you need. If you choose to go on to college, you will have even more choices. The last chapters in this book will outline careers in child care that are available to those with a college degree or more.

Salary

Everyone wants to make a lot of money, but this should not be your number one concern when you first start out. It's important to understand that you may not make a lot of money right away. Sometimes gaining good experience is more important than how much you earn. It is a good idea, however, to have a certain salary range in mind when looking for a job. A good way to figure out the right salary for you is to calculate your living expenses. Are you going to have to pay car insurance? Do not forget to include rent, groceries, travel expenses, and social activities. Once you have made a list of all your expenses, you can estimate how much money you will need to earn each week.

Some jobs pay better than others. Keep in mind that no matter what job you start out with, it may take some time to work your way up, both in responsibility and salary.

Working Environment

Another important thing to consider is your working environment. Do you want to work in an office? Often, working with children requires you to be outdoors, in classrooms, libraries, or playrooms. Another issue that comes up when working with children is that you are sometimes the only adult around. Some people don't mind working alone, while others prefer to have people their own age to talk to.

Do you know what kind of hours you would like to work? For example, many nannies and baby-sitters may have to

While you are still in school, consider working part-time, perhaps at an after-school center, play group, or community organization.

work a lot of nights. Teachers only work until 3:00 PM, but they tend to take home a lot of work and spend an incredible amount of time preparing lessons and meeting with parents. If you are considering part-time work, after-school centers, play groups, and community organizations, such as Big Brothers/Big Sisters and the local YMCA, may offer flexible hours.

Exploring Your Options

2

Once you have decided that you want to work with children, you are ready to narrow down your job search and choose a career path that is right for you.

Being a Baby-Sitter

Baby-sitting usually involves working with a small number of children in their own home. This job may require some light cooking and housekeeping, but your main responsibility is the safety and well-being of the children. Baby-sitting is something you can start doing while you are still in high school. The best way to get a baby-sitting job is through friends and family. It might be a good idea to volunteer to watch a little brother or sister so you can get some experience before looking for a baby-sitting job.

Baby-sitters usually get paid by the hour, and rates vary depending on your experience, how many children you are watching, and whether you are baby-sitting at night

Baby-sitting offers flexible hours, decent pay, and the opportunity to develop a close relationship with a child.

while the children are asleep, or during the day when you are responsible for entertaining them. Rates generally range between $5 and $10 per hour.

Baby-sitting can be very fulfilling. The hours are usually flexible, and you get to develop a close relationship with a child. Some parents only need baby-sitters for a few hours, which may be good if you have another job or are still in school. Other people need baby-sitters full-time. If you work a set schedule each week, it may be more convenient to get paid on a weekly basis.

Household Child Care Workers

Household child care workers, or nannies, spend a lot of time with the family they work for. They take care of children, cook meals, and do housework. Many nannies live with the family. They are given room and board plus a salary. Most nannies work at least five days a week. Some nannies live in their own homes and commute to work each day. A nanny may be responsible for picking up children from school, taking them to doctor appointments and after-school activities, preparing their meals, and bathing them.

While no specific training is required to be a nanny, it is a good idea to take a course in first aid. Courses in cooking and child development are also available. These classes can usually be found at local community centers. Nannies generally earn between $10,000 and $15,000 a year. One way to become a nanny is through an au pair service. Au pairs do the same work as nannies, only they usually work in a foreign country. Au pair agencies match people with families in other countries. This gives the au pair the opportunity to live in a new place and experience a new culture while working. Since au pairs are almost always live-ins, they do not have to worry about room and board. Au pairs usually stay with a family for about a year.

Day Care Center Workers

Raoul had been a camp counselor for the past three years. He enjoyed working with large groups of children. This June he would be graduating from high school. He had known for years that he wanted to pursue a career in child care. He had heard that there was an opening at one of the neighborhood day care centers. Raoul had always worked with older children. He understood that working in a day care center would be a lot different. The children would be younger and would probably require a lot more care.

Raoul submitted his application and went on an interview. Two weeks later he got a call from the administrator saying he had gotten the job. He was told that his responsibilities would include feeding the children and changing diapers. Raoul decided that even if he had to change dirty diapers, working in a day care center would be very rewarding.

Your school may have a bulletin board or employment office with listings of jobs.

With more and more parents working full-time, the demand for responsible day care workers is increasing. Day care workers play an important part in a child's life. They spend many hours a day tending to a child's needs, nurturing the child, and helping him or her grow. A child in day care gets to socialize and interact with other children. This helps the child develop and learn skills like sharing.

While most of a day care worker's time is spent with the children, he or she also has informal meetings with parents to discuss each child's progress and needs.

Children in day care range in age from infant to six years old. Part-time and full-time work is available for day care workers. Being able to work with large groups of children and keeping them busy with creative and educational activities are important parts of this job. Little prior experience is required. The average salary ranges from about $12,000 to $15,000 a year for full-time workers. Benefits vary but are generally minimal. Some employers offer insurance, vacation time, and free child care for workers who have their own children.

Teacher's Aides

Another career opportunity to explore in the field of education is the job of teacher's aide. Most teacher's aides work part-time, and education requirements range from a high school diploma to some college training. Teacher's aides tutor and assist children, often helping out not only in the classroom but also in the cafeteria and schoolyard. They also perform general administrative tasks for teachers. Teacher's aides earn between $8 and $10 per hour.

Volunteer Programs

If you are interested in helping children and would like to get some experience, another option to explore is volunteering. There are many programs dedicated to improving the health and well-being of children. Some of these programs allow you to work one-on-one with a child. In other programs you might be one of many counselors assisting with field trips, educational projects, and sports activities. These programs are a good way to find out if you are interested in pursuing a career in child care. After volunteering for a while you may decide to become a full-time staff member, helping out with administration, planning trips, or recruiting volunteers.

Salary varies depending on what foundation you work for and what position you choose. For many of these positions, a high school diploma is sufficient. For some jobs, like being a caseworker—in which you visit families and assess a child's needs—a college degree is necessary. Some of these programs are Big Brothers/Big Sisters, Boys and Girls Club, Save the Children, and the YMCA.

Teacher's aides tutor and assist children, helping out not only in the classroom but often in the cafeteria and schoolyard as well.

Hands-On Experience 3

Cyrus was working in an after-school center part-time. He had always loved children and had planned to pursue a career in child care. He thought it would be a good idea to get some solid experience working with children before graduating from high school. This would give Cyrus a better idea of what type of job he would like to have in the future.

Cyrus had two younger brothers and enjoyed playing with them, teaching them new things and spending time with them. He had done some baby-sitting for the family down the block but had never been responsible for a large group of children until now.

Working in the after-school center was harder than he thought. Every child seemed to need his attention at all times. Even if he wasn't in the mood, he had to act happy and have a lot of patience. Cyrus always thought working with children would be easy. Soon he began to

Having younger siblings—playing with them and teaching them new things—is excellent preparation for a career in child care.

settle into a routine and learned to handle the children's needs one at a time. The more time he spent with the children, the easier and more rewarding his job became.

Cyrus was glad he was getting this experience now. When he applied for a full-time job after high school, he would know exactly what to expect.

Things You Can Do Now

There are many jobs and career paths for people interested in working with children. Some jobs require a lot of training and education, while others do not. Before pursuing a long-term career in one of these fields, it is a good idea to do some research and then set some goals.

A great way to do some research is by gaining hands-on experience. Volunteering in local community centers, as mentioned in the previous chapter, will put you on the right track. Once you have done some volunteer work with children, you will have a better understanding of what you are interested in doing.

Internships are another way to gain experience. As an intern, you work a set amount of time each week at a place similar to where you think you would like to work in the future. Some internships pay while others do not. Internships are a great way to get experience. You get to see first-hand how things are done in certain jobs and what kind of environment you might be working in. The best part is, you're still at the point in your life where it is easy to change your mind about what you want to do. For example, you may think you want to be a social worker, but after a six-month internship you may realize it is not the right career path for you.

You may feel that there is not enough

time in your schedule right now to do a lot of planning for your future. There are many things you can do that don't take up a lot of time and will still give you good solid experience. During the school year you can go to local elementary schools to see if they need tutors. Remember, even if math isn't your best subject now, you can still help a first grader with his or her math homework.

Many schools also have programs where you can read to a child for an hour once a week. Not only are you giving a child the attention he or she might need, but you are also gaining experience. This experience will give you an edge, so to speak, when you apply for a job in child care.

Another way to gain experience is to check out events at your local public library. Many children's libraries are always looking for volunteers to read to children during story hour. You can also help children pick out their favorite books to take home. Talk to the librarian to set up a schedule. Sometimes it's hard to think about the future when you have so many other things on your mind. You have school and homework, chores and responsibilities. You shouldn't worry or feel

As a library volunteer, you can help children pick out their favorite books to take home.

overwhelmed about what you are going to do with the rest of your life. It's important to take things one step at a time. If you feel as though you have absolutely no room in your schedule to dedicate to your future career, the best thing to do is to concentrate on your schoolwork and get good grades. This will give you the opportunity to pursue whatever career you choose later.

Summertime Experience

Drew had a very busy schedule during the year. Besides keeping up with his studies, he had to go home every day after school and help his mom take care of his two younger sisters. He loved his family and enjoyed spending time with them, but he also wished he could get a job so he could have some work experience when he graduated from high school. He realized that there was just no way that he could keep up his grades, help his mom out, and work part-time. His school guidance counselor suggested that he look for a summer job instead. That way he wouldn't have the stress of worrying about schoolwork. If he started looking for a summer job in April or May, he'd be working in a great place by July.

If you find that you don't have any extra time during the school year, the summer is a great time to pursue your interests. Summer camps are always looking for responsible high school students to become counselors. This is an exciting summer job. You get to spend a lot of time outdoors, playing sports, going to parks, swimming, and even going on boat rides. Plus, the best part is, you get paid for doing all of this. There are two types of summer camps: sleep-away camp and day camp.

Working in a sleep-away camp usually means leaving home for the summer and sleeping in a cabin with your camp group. There are usually a few counselors for each group, so you can depend on others to help. Counselors have to help children get dressed, comfort them when they miss home, and try to make sure they are having a good time. Day camp counselors work a full day and then go home. Day camps go on a lot of trips to places like the zoo, ballparks, and the aquarium. It's important to keep an eye on your group at all times and to count them every time you get on and off the bus to make sure no one is missing.

A good way to find camps that are hiring is to go through the yellow pages and look for the day camps in your area. You can also ask friends or family members who have children where they send their kids to camp. When you call up the camp, explain that you are looking for a summer job and ask if there are any positions available. Don't wait until the summer to call, though. Most camps hire their staffs by April or May.

Another good way to get experience during the summer is to find a part-time baby-sitting job. You can baby-sit a few

Day camp counselors go on a lot of trips, taking kids to places such as the zoo, ballparks, and the aquarium.

hours a week, at night, or on the weekends. This will give you an idea of what it is like to be responsible for a child. Ask friends, neighbors, and family, or post signs in school or at your local community center to let people know that you're interested in this type of job. Remember, baby-sitting is a big responsibility because you are the only one in charge. Baby-sitting is not the time to chat on the phone with friends. However, if you are baby-sitting at night and the child is asleep, you can ask the parents if they mind if you watch television or catch up on your studies.

It may seem hard to plan for your future now, but the more experience you have, the better off you will be. Even if you plan to be a pediatrician or a child psychologist, tutoring a child, reading a child stories, or volunteering in a community center now is very important. You may think that being a teacher is the perfect job for you, but unless you actually spend time with children, it can be hard to tell. Setting short-term goals and testing the waters now can save you a lot of time later.

A World of Opportunities

4

There is a long list of jobs available in the field of child care. After you have made a commitment to dedicating your life to the happiness and well-being of children, you may want to explore long-term, higher-paying careers. Because children have many needs, there are numerous job opportunities.

Teachers

Tara was a fifth-grade teacher at the neighborhood elementary school. She loved working with children, preparing exciting lesson plans, reading the children's papers, and coming up with new classroom activities. Tara taught all the subjects except arts and crafts and health. As a teacher, Tara worked until 3:00 PM every day. She got vacation when the kids got vacation, and summers off. Tara loved her job, but it was very challenging. She spent a lot of time after school grading papers and preparing lessons. Even when Tara was having a bad day or was feeling a little sick, she had

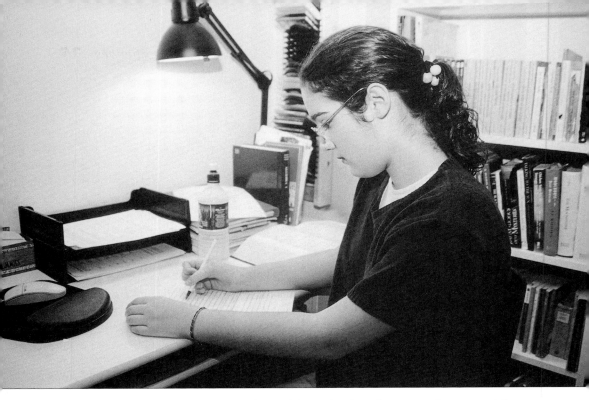

Students need to be challenged by schoolwork, so teachers must be inventive when coming up with new classroom activities.

to keep a smile on her face and act interested in the lesson she was teaching. Tara had to deal with kids who weren't always interested in what she was discussing in the classroom. This required a lot of patience. Tara also had to talk to parents about a child's progress. It was hard work, but when the children in Tara's class showed enthusiasm for their work and scored high marks on tests, Tara knew she had chosen the right career.

A college education is required to become a teacher. Most teachers go on to get a master's degree and a teaching license. A master's degree is a type of degree you get if you continue to go to school after graduating from college. Requirements for a teaching license vary from state to state. All states do require a completed teacher training program with a certain number of education credits and supervised practice teaching. Practice teaching means that you teach in a classroom with the supervision of a licensed teacher.

The average starting salary for public elementary and secondary school teachers is between $27,000 and $40,000. Teachers usually get a good benefits package, including medical insurance and vacation time. Teachers who work in private schools make less money, and while they are still required to have a college education, a license isn't always necessary. Private schools pay from $12,000 to $25,000 to start, and benefits aren't always as good as in public schools. Working in a private school does have its advantages, though. Classrooms are usually smaller, creating more one-on-one time between students and teachers.

Special Education Teachers

Special education teachers work with children who have disabilities, including mental retardation, emotional problems, or speech and hearing impairments. Special education teachers design activities suited to a child's needs and abilities. Special education classes are usually smaller than general education classes, and the children get more individual attention. Some special education teachers work with teachers in general education classrooms, adapting the curriculum to help certain students. Others work in a resource room, providing students in a regular classroom with extra help and attention.

A special education teacher must identify a child's needs and provide him or her with the resources he or she needs to do well in school. Special education teachers often develop meaningful relationships with their students as they watch them grow and succeed in school. This type of job requires a teaching license and usually requires training in a specialty, such as behavior disorders. Salary and education requirements are the same as for general education teachers.

Guidance Counselors

Guidance counselors help children deal with personal problems they are having at school and at home. Counselors also help students

Getting children involved in playing challenging games is one way to boost their self-confidence.

understand their abilities and their weaknesses so that they know what areas they have to work harder at developing. Guidance counselors work the same hours as teachers. A college degree is required, and most guidance counselors have a master's degree. All school counselors must have State School Counseling Certification. This may require some teaching experience. Starting salary for a school guidance counselor is anywhere from $30,000 to $50,000.

Social Workers

Remi always liked helping people. In high school, he volunteered at the after-school cen-

ter. He was always very understanding and knew how to relate well to children. He loved making children feel better by telling jokes or just listening to them. Sometimes the children came from families who were going through difficult times. These kids often had a hard time adjusting in the classroom. Remi tried to boost their self-confidence by playing games the kids were good at and by tutoring them in difficult subjects. Before graduating from high school, Remi knew he wanted to be a social worker. This was a good way to continue to make a difference in the lives of children.

Social workers help people deal with issues that affect their daily life, such as personal, family, or environmental problems. Sometimes social workers assist children who have been victims of child abuse. A social worker can work in hospitals, schools, clinics, or public agencies. Sometimes social workers go to a family's home. Social workers who work with children counsel them and help the child's family find further resources to assist them with their problems. Part of a social worker's job may be to give advice to parents on how to care for their child.

Social workers work full-time, adjusting their schedule to meet with clients. This means that some evening and weekend work may be required. There are also part-time positions available for social workers, usually in nonprofit agencies.

This type of work is satisfying because you can have a positive impact on a child's life. However, being a social worker can be frustrating and emotionally draining. Sometimes you have to deal with people who don't really want your help. A college degree is the minimum requirement for an entry-level position. Majoring in psychology or sociology as an undergraduate is helpful. A master's degree is required for jobs in public agencies. However, some places will hire you and may even assist you with tuition while you are studying for your master's. Depending on your degree and whether you work for a hospital, school, or a public or private agency, the annual salary for an entry-level social worker is between $25,000 and $50,000.

Child Psychologists

Child psychologists work with a child and his or her parents to help deal with some of the problems the child is experiencing. These problems can include behavioral problems, learning difficulties, and trouble adjusting to new situations. Working conditions depend on whether a person works in a school or clinic, or has a private practice. People in private practice often work evening and weekend hours so clients can easily see them. Psychologists who work in schools and clinics work regular hours. Most psychologists have a doctoral degree, known as a Ph.D. A lot of people have full-time jobs while studying for a Ph.D. Most people teach, counsel, or do research while going to school at night to get their degree. People with a bachelor's degree in psychology can assist psychologists.

Child psychologists have to be very mature and able to deal with other people's problems. They have to be calm and patient and good listeners. Depending on what kind of degree you have and whether you work in a school, clinic, or private practice, you can earn anywhere from $30,000 to over $100,000, though it takes years for a psychologist to earn over $100,000. Most people start out in agencies while developing a private practice.

Speech Pathologists

Speech pathologists treat people with language and voice disorders. They work with people, often children, who have trouble making speech sounds. Some children stutter or have a lisp and need help with these impediments. Speech pathologists use written and oral tests to help them understand a child's difficulty. Sometimes they help teach patients to make sounds and improve their language skills. They often work closely with doctors and psychologists to help develop the best treatment plan for a patient. Speech pathologists tend to work in schools with both individuals and groups of students. They also counsel parents and assist teachers with special classroom activities. Like most jobs in child care, this one requires a lot of patience and concentration. Progress is often slow for children with speech difficulties.

Most speech pathologists work about forty hours a week in a comfortable office environment. In order to be a speech pathologist, you need a master's degree in speech. To get a license, a person must first have supervised clinical experience and nine months of work experience after graduation, and must pass a national exam. People with a bachelor's degree can work in schools with students who have communication problems while studying for their master's. Speech pathologists earn between $35,000 and $60,000 a year.

Audiologists

An audiologist is someone who works with people who have hearing problems. Half of all audiologists work in schools, using special instruments to check a child's hearing. A person can be born deaf or may lose his or her hearing after being exposed to a viral infection or loud noise. Audiologists can teach a child how to lip-read and can recommend or fit a person for a hearing aid.

Audiologists usually work in an office environment about forty hours a week. A master's degree is generally required for this type of work. As with speech pathologists, to get a license, audiologists have to work a certain amount of hours, usually 300 to 375, in a clinic. They also have to pass a national test. Audiologists have to be kind and supportive to both the child and his or her parents. Salaries vary depending on the state and type of place where the audiologist works. They generally earn between $30,000 and $60,000 a year.

Pediatricians

Lydia was in her first year of medical school. She had always loved science, and this had been her dream. She was premed in college, meaning that most of her college courses helped her prepare for medical school. Even with all this preparation, medical school was hard. Lydia tried to stay in touch with her friends and family, but most of her time was dedicated to her studies. Still, she was happy with her decision to become a doctor.

At first, Lydia didn't know what type of doctor she wanted to become. There were so many choices. She didn't have to decide for a few more years, but after thinking about it for a while, she realized she had the ability to be a great pediatrician. She loved children and had a great bedside manner. She also knew how tough it could be to deal with patients who couldn't always tell you what was wrong. Lydia understood that she still had time to change her mind down the road, but she was pretty confident that being a pediatrician was the right career for her.

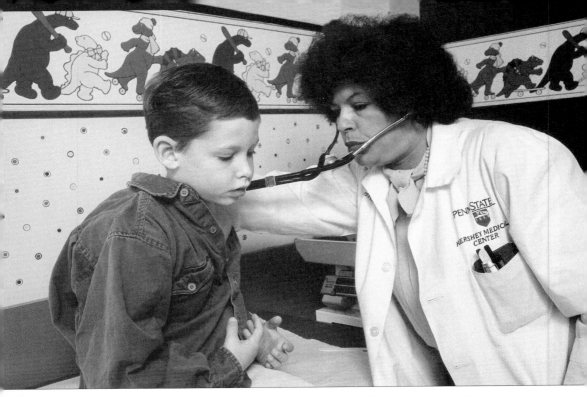

Pediatricians often work with sick and sometimes scared kids, so they must be patient and understanding.

Pediatricians are doctors who specialize in children's medicine. Some pediatricians work in a hospital, while others have a private practice. They take care of the sick and give annual checkups to all patients. Many pediatricians work long hours. Sometimes they work nights and weekends so they can see patients. Becoming a pediatrician is hard work and requires years of education, but it is also a very fulfilling job. Helping children feel better and reassuring worried parents are two things that make this a great career. Schooling includes four years of medical school and three to eight years of internships in a hospital. This is a long-term commitment, but well worth it. You have to be very motivated and able to handle pressure well. A pediatrician works with sick, often scared kids, so you have to have a good bedside manner and a friendly disposition. Physicians have one of the highest paying jobs out there. This is because it is also one of the hardest. Physicians earn between $160,000 to $300,000 a year, while those working in private practice can earn even more.

The jobs mentioned in this chapter require a lot of hard work. Right now you may not be sure if you want to make that type of commitment and pursue such long-term goals. This is perfectly understandable. Even if you don't know exactly what you want to do right now, preparing for your future is still very important. If you know you want to work with children, you can start off by researching colleges that have good programs in the sciences. Even if you change your mind later on, you will still be on the road to success.

Getting Started   5

Sharese was graduating from high school in less than a month. She had done some basic research on careers in child care and decided that she wanted to be a teacher's aide. She knew a lot about the position and realized it would be a good place to start should she decide to go back to school and become a teacher later on.

Sharese prepared herself for this job by getting some experience while still in high school. She baby-sat on Saturday nights and tutored third-graders after school. One Thursday a month she read to children at the local library. Sharese had experience working with individual children and large groups. She was confident that she could get a job as a teacher's aide. The only problem was, Sharese had never been on an interview before, didn't have a résumé prepared, and didn't really know who to contact about getting a job. Sharese wasn't even sure where jobs for teacher's aides were advertised.

The first thing you need to do when looking for a job is to prepare a résumé.

Writing Your Résumé

Deciding on the type of career you want takes a lot of thought, but it is only the first step toward getting a good job. The very first thing you need to do once you've decided what kind of job you want is to prepare a résumé. A résumé is a piece of paper that tells about your experience, accomplishments, and skills. Many people just out of high school or college don't have a lot of experience. This is perfectly understandable, and job interviewers are aware of this.

Your résumé should be one typed page.

This piece of paper represents who you are. It is the first thing a potential employer sees, so make sure that there are no mistakes. Read it over carefully and have at least two other people look at it. Ask a parent or teacher to check it over for grammar and spelling.

There are many different ways to write a résumé, but it's important to keep it simple. Use white paper. Include your name, address, and phone number at the top. Put the type of education you have first. Write down the name of the last school you attended, the address, and the year you graduated.

Next, write about your job experience. Don't forget to include internships or

Example:
The Acorn After-School Program, New York, New York
Counselor, *September 1998 to Present*
- Responsible for organizing after-school activities, including ball games and arts and crafts.
- Help children with homework.
- Serve snacks.

special programs you have participated in. Your last or current job should be listed first. Remember, be brief and to the point.

Cover Letter

You should include a short cover letter with every résumé you send out. This letter should say which job you are applying for and why you are a good candidate. You don't have to go into detail in a cover letter. The purpose of one of these letters is to briefly introduce yourself and to describe the skills and experience you have. Try to keep this letter approximately two to three paragraphs long. There are many books at your local library explaining how to write a résumé and cover letter. Look through a few of these to find a style that best suits you.

Networking and Contacts

Networking means talking to people and putting the word out that you're looking for a job. There are many ways to network. Friends, neighbors, school counselors, and just about anyone else can help you find the right job. You never know who might have a friend or relative

Take notes when speaking to potential employers. Jot down the date of the call and the name of the person you spoke to.

working in a place similar to where you want to work.

It is important to follow up on all leads, even if they don't seem to be exactly what you're looking for. Sometimes it's hard to talk to people you don't know, but if you are polite and friendly, most people will be responsive and helpful. It's important to find people who can pass along job information for you. Keep track of all the people you speak to. The easiest way to do this is to keep a small notebook of your job search progress. Write down the date you spoke with the person, who referred you to him or her, and how he or she was able to assist you. Once you find a job, keep the notebook in a safe place. You may be tempted to throw it away, but the next time you are looking for a job, if you still have these contacts, you'll be one step ahead of the game.

Job Hunting

There are many ways to go about finding a job. The first place to start is school. If you have a job center or career counselors at your school, you can explain your interests and ask if they can assist you in your job search. Some schools post job openings on a bulletin board. Another good way to search for a job is through the local newspaper. The classifieds are small ads placed in the newspaper that include a brief job description along with a phone number and an address telling you where to send your résumé. For jobs in child care, you can look in the classifieds under specific job titles and also under Child Care.

Employment offices are another place to look for jobs. The people who work in these places are trained to help you find a job. You can find the employment office nearest you by looking in the phone book or by asking a career counselor. Going to your local library and browsing through the career section can be very helpful. There are tons of books that explain everything about how to do a job search. Finally, the Internet can help you find a great job. There are many job listings on the Web. Just type in keywords like "Jobs," "Careers," or "Child Care." You can also type in the exact title of the job you want.

Don't expect to find a job right away.

Always dress appropriately for an interview.

Sometimes it can take months before you even get an interview. Finding a job takes a lot of time and patience.

Job Applications

Many places may require that you fill out an application. An application usually asks for basic information about yourself. This could include things like your phone number, address, Social Security number, and prior job information. There may also be a few situational, or job-related, questions. If possible, ask if you can take the application home with you so you can take your time filling it out. You should carry a picture identification with you in case a copy of it is required.

The Interview

Going on an interview can be very intimidating. But if you are prepared, you have nothing to worry about. Once you have been notified that you have been chosen for an interview, you should find out as much information as you can about the place. You can do this by going on-line. If the place where you'll be interviewing is a big company, there may be a lot of information available. Your local library is another great resource.

When you go on an interview, you should be prepared with a list of questions about the job. Asking questions on an interview shows that you are interested in the position. Some basic questions you may want to ask include: What are the hours? What age group will I be working with? What are my responsibilities? Although you may be tempted, you don't have to discuss salary until you are offered the job. At that point, you can decide if the job pays enough.

A good way to prepare for an interview is by practicing answering and asking questions. You may be asked why you feel this is the right job for you. An interviewer may want to know about your experience, your hobbies, and your strengths and weaknesses.

Always dress appropriately for an interview. You should look neat and clean. Try to arrive at least ten minutes early for an interview, and never be late. When you meet the person who will be interviewing you, shake hands firmly and wait to be directed to the room where the interview will take place. Be kind and courteous to everyone, smile, and act friendly. When interviewing with someone, look the person in the eye and think about your answers before you speak. When the interview is over, thank the person for his or her time.

It's a good idea to follow up with a thank-you letter. This should be a brief letter thanking the person who interviewed you. Mention the job you are applying for and close by saying you hope to hear from him or her soon. If you don't hear anything back from the person who interviewed you for a few days, you can call to follow up. Just because you don't hear anything immediately doesn't mean that they aren't interested. Most people are very busy, and job interviews are only one of the many tasks they have to attend to during the course of the day.

Finding the right job is hard work but well worth the effort. The field of child care is growing, and the opportunities are endless. Setting goals, volunteering to gain experience, and doing some research will help you land your dream job. If you reach for the stars, you can have a meaningful career helping children, reaching out to them, and watching them develop and grow.

Glossary

au pair A person who comes from another country to be a live-in nanny for about a year.

classifieds Newspaper and magazine notices that advertise employment in different fields.

concept An idea or thought.

doctoral degree The highest degree awarded by universities.

impediment A speech defect.

interaction Involvement with other people.

internship A job, sometimes unpaid, taken to gain experience in a certain field.

master's degree An advanced degree awarded by a university, obtained after a bachelor's degree.

networking Developing contacts and obtaining information.

personality traits Distinguishing characteristics of a person.

Where to Go for Help

In the United States

American Red Cross
18th and F Streets NW
Washington, DC 20006

Best Domestic Service Agency
310 Madison Avenue, Suite 1517
New York, NY 10017
(212) 685-0351

Big Brothers and Sisters of America
230 North 13th Street
Philadelphia, PA 19107
(215) 567-7000
Web site: http://www.bbsa.org

Childcare Assistance Network
P.O. Box 502
San Clemente, CA 92672
(714) 506-3525

Child Care Information Center
301 Maple Avenue West
Suite 601
Vienna, VA 22180

National Center for Early Childhood Workforce
733 15th Street NW, Suite 1037
Washington, DC 20005
(202) 737-7700

YMCA of the USA
101 North Wacker Drive
Chicago, IL 60606
Web site: http://www.ymca.net

In Canada

Association of Early Childhood Educators
Ontario Provincial Officer
40 Orchard View Boulevard, Suite 211
Toronto, ON M4R 1B9
(416) 487-3157

Au Pair D.G. International
1611 Des Lilas
St. Lazare
Quebec J7T 2R5
(450) 510-1602

Big Brothers and Sisters of Canada
3228 South Service Road
Burlington, ON L7N3H8
(800) 263-9133
Web site: http://www.bbsc.ca/index.html

Canadian Au Pairs
5259 Sooke Road
Sooke, BC V0S 1N0
(250) 642-0298
E-mail: canadianaupairs@hotmail.com

For Further Reading

Barkin, Carol, and Elizabeth James. *The New Complete Babysitter's Handbook.* New York: Clarion Books, 1995.

Bumgarner, Marlene Anne. *Working with School-Age Children.* Mountain View, CA: Mayfield Printing and Office Equipment Publishers, 1999.

Dowd, Tom, and Susan E. O'Kane. *Effective Skills for Child-Care Workers.* Boys Town, NE: Boys Town Press, 1995.

Eberts, Marjorie, and Margaret Gisler. *Careers in Child Care.* Lincolnwood, IL: VGM Career Horizons, 1994.

Herr, Judy. *Working with Young Children.* Tinley Park, IL: Goodheart-Willcox Company, 1999.

Krueger, Mark A. *Job Satisfaction for Child Care Workers.* Washington, DC: Child Care Welfare League of America, 1996.

Quinlan, Kathryn A. *Child Care Worker (Careers Without College)*. Mankato, MN: Capstone Press, January 1999.

Sommers, Annie Leah. *Effective Communication at School and at Work*. New York: Rosen Publishing Group, 2000.

Weintraub, Aileen. *Everything You Need to Know About Being a Baby-Sitter*. New York: Rosen Publishing Group, 1999.

Wittenberg, Renee. *Opportunities in Child Care*. Lincolnwood, IL: VGM Career Horizons, 1994.

Index

About the Author

Aileen Weintraub is an editor and writer residing in Brooklyn, New York. This is her third book for young adults. She is currently working on a series of children's books.

Photo Credits

Cover and interior shots by Ira Fox except pp. 2, 37, 50 by Thaddeus Harden; p. 15 by Lauren Piperno; p. 17 by Brian Silak; p. 20 by Kim Sonsky and Matthew Baumann; p. 31 © Superstock; p. 44 by Kelly Hahn.

Layout

Geri Giordano